AMAZING ENGINEERING JOBS

COLIN HYNSON

WAYLAND

First published in Great Britain
in 2016 by Wayland
Copyright © Wayland, 2016
All rights reserved

Editor: Victoria Brooker
Produced by Tall Tree Ltd
Editor: Jon Richards
Designer: Darren Jordan

ISBN: 978 1 5263 0008 9
10 9 8 7 6 5 4 3 2 1

Wayland
An imprint of Hachette
Children's Group
Part of Hodder and Stoughton
Carmelite House
50 Victoria Embankment
London EC4Y 0DZ

An Hachette UK Company
www.hachette.co.uk
www.hachettechildrens.co.uk

Printed and bound in China

The website addresses (URLs) included in this
book were valid at the time of going to press.
However, it is possible that contents or addresses
may have changed since the publication of this
book. No responsibility for any such changes can
be accepted by either the author or the Publisher.

Picture credits

1, 26bl courtesy of NASA, 2, 12–13 Dreamstime.com/Mikhail Druzhinin,
3, 23b Dreamstime.com/Piccaya, 4–5 Dreamstime.com/Gleres, 5tr
Dreamstime.com/Lunamarina, 5cr Dreamstime.com/Alexander
Sandvoss, 6–7 Dreamstime.com/Freestyleimages, 7tl Dreamstime.com/
Viachelav Iacobchuk, 8cl Dreamstime.com/Cylonphoto, 8–9
Dreamstime.com/Stockr, 10cl Dreamstime.com/Delfinista, 10–11
Dreamstime.com/Alexander Sandvoss, 11tr Dreamstime.com/Ivan23g,
12cl Dreamstime.com/Belahoche, 14cl Citypeek Creative Commons
Sharealike, 14–15 Dreamstime.com/Pichit Boonhuad, 16bl Dreamstime.
com/Jasminko Ibrakovic, 16–17 Dreamstime.com/James Frecker, 18bl,
31br Dreamstime.com/Bai Xuejia, 18–19 Dreamstime.com/ Péter
Gudella, 19cl Dreamstime.com/Piero Crucciati, 20–21 Dreamstime.com/
Maren Winter, 22cl Dreamstime.com/ProductionPerig, 24bl FlickrLickr
Creative Commons Sharealike, 24–25 Dreamstime.com/Grigor
Atanasov, 26–27 Dreamstime.com/Boarding1now, 27tl courtesy of
NASA, 28–29 Dreamstime.com/Martine De Graaf

CONTENTS

ENGINEERING

JOBS IN ENGINEERING

A QUALIFICATION IN ENGINEERING CAN TAKE YOU FROM THE DEPTHS OF THE EARTH TO TOWERS THAT SOAR HIGH INTO THE SKY.

Welcome to the world of working in engineering. Studying engineering is really worthwhile, because it opens doors to a whole range of interesting, exciting and unusual jobs — amazing jobs in engineering.

Studying engineering doesn't mean you'll be stuck on a building site. There are jobs in robotics, motor racing and 3-D printing, to name a few. Find out what each job is all about, as well as the rewards of doing the job.

▼ Creating a terrifying theme park ride requires a detailed understanding of forces and the strength of materials.

SUBJECTS AND QUALIFICATIONS

For each job, we've shown what subjects you can study as you move through education from school to university and beyond, and what further training you would need. These are quite general because what you study for a particular qualification will change depending on which country you are in.

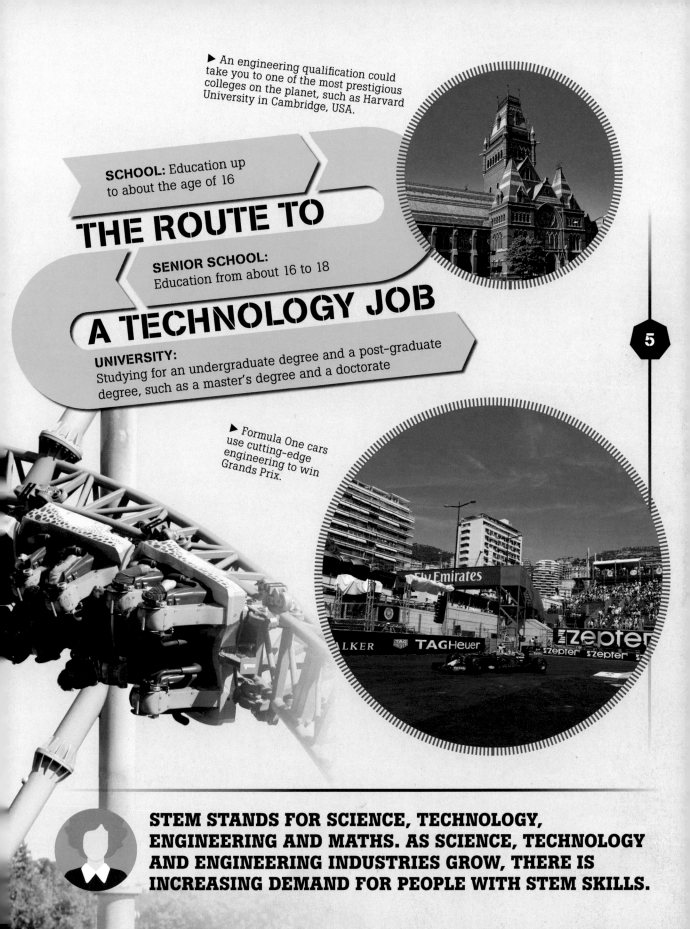

▶ An engineering qualification could take you to one of the most prestigious colleges on the planet, such as Harvard University in Cambridge, USA.

SCHOOL: Education up to about the age of 16

THE ROUTE TO

SENIOR SCHOOL: Education from about 16 to 18

A TECHNOLOGY JOB

UNIVERSITY: Studying for an undergraduate degree and a post-graduate degree, such as a master's degree and a doctorate

▶ Formula One cars use cutting-edge engineering to win Grands Prix.

STEM STANDS FOR SCIENCE, TECHNOLOGY, ENGINEERING AND MATHS. AS SCIENCE, TECHNOLOGY AND ENGINEERING INDUSTRIES GROW, THERE IS INCREASING DEMAND FOR PEOPLE WITH STEM SKILLS.

PRINTING IN 3-D

THIS TECHNOLOGY ALLOWS YOU TO MAKE WHAT YOU WANT, WHEN YOU WANT IT.

Also known as 'additive manufacturing', 3-D printing allows businesses to create new products easily, without having to build expensive prototypes. The method can also be used to make a small number of the product to see if people are interested in buying it. Even though it is still quite a new industry, 3-D printing is being used in a wide range of industries, including car and aircraft building, and even creating new body parts.

> 3-D PRINTING USES A WIDE RANGE OF MATERIALS INCLUDING PLASTIC, CLAY, METAL, RUBBER AND EVEN FOOD.

One:

◀ A digital model of the item is created on computer before the 3-D printers get to work.

WHAT YOU DO

Working as a 3-D printing engineer, you will be involved in the process of creating a new product from start to finish. You'll spend much of your day making sure that the 3-D printer is ready to start working and that the materials being used are also available. You'll be working as part of a team including designers and computer coders who use Computer–Aided Design (CAD) software.

WHERE YOU WORK

At the moment most people in 3-D printing work with engineering companies or in aerospace and healthcare. However, the range of businesses that are looking to use 3-D printing is expanding fast. One growth area is in electrical engineering where 3-D printing can be used to create electrical circuits.

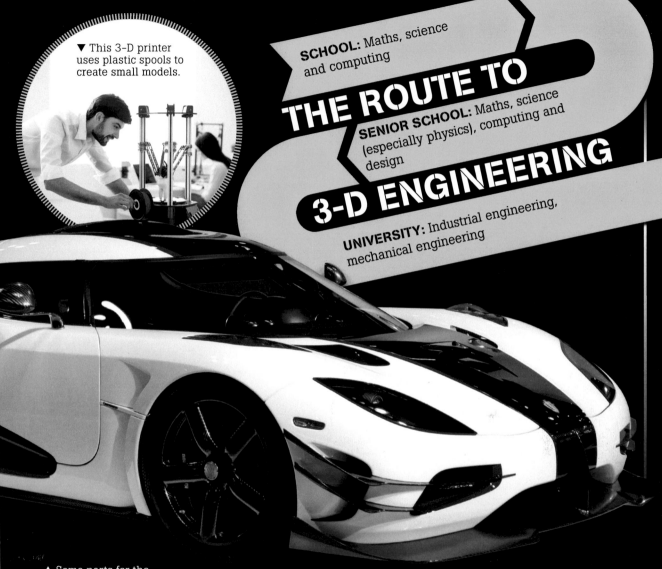

▼ This 3-D printer uses plastic spools to create small models.

THE ROUTE TO 3-D ENGINEERING

SCHOOL: Maths, science and computing

SENIOR SCHOOL: Maths, science (especially physics), computing and design

UNIVERSITY: Industrial engineering, mechanical engineering

▲ Some parts for the Koenigsegg One:1 supercar were created using 3-D printing.

NASA IS SEEING IF 3-D PRINTING CAN CREATE ENTIRE MEALS FOR ASTRONAUTS. THIS MEANS THAT THEY CAN MAKE SURE THAT ASTRONAUTS ARE GETTING TASTY AND NUTRITIOUS FOOD.

GREEN ENGINEERING

PLAY YOUR PART IN SAVING THE PLANET AND USE YOUR ENGINEERING QUALIFICATIONS TO KEEP THINGS GREEN.

One of the greatest challenges facing us all today is the issue of climate change. We are producing millions of tonnes of greenhouse gases every year and many people believe that it's changing our climate, making our planet warmer. To try and reduce the impact, many countries are developing renewable sources of energy, producing electricity from wind, sunlight and water.

◀ Engineers inspect the huge turbines in a hydroelectric power plant.

WHAT YOU DO

As a renewable engineer you will spend some of your time working in a laboratory designing and researching renewable energy projects. This will mean creating computer models and carrying out experiments. The rest of your time will be working outside choosing places to build a wind turbine or a solar farm and then returning when building starts. If you're designing an off-shore wind turbine then this will mean going out to sea.

AN AREA OF RENEWABLE ENGINEERING THAT NEEDS MORE RESEARCH IS IN THE STORAGE OF ENERGY. AT THE MOMENT, STORING POWER IS NOT EASY, AND COMPANIES ARE LOOKING TO DEVELOP BETTER WAYS OF DOING THIS.

THE IVANPAH SOLAR ELECTRIC GENERATING SYSTEM IN CALIFORNIA, USA, COVERS 1,500 HECTARES AND CAN GENERATE ENOUGH POWER FOR NEARLY 140,000 HOMES.

9

◀ Gigantic turbines stand high above the ground to make the most of the wind.

WHERE YOU WORK

Engineers working in renewable energy will work for businesses that design, build and install the machinery needed to capture energy. Many businesses tend to concentrate on just one kind of renewable energy, so you can choose whether you want to work in wind, solar or hydropower.

THE ROUTE TO

SCHOOL: Maths, science and computing

SENIOR SCHOOL: Maths, science (especially physics), computing and engineering

RENEWABLE

UNIVERSITY: Mechanical engineering or electrical engineering. Some universities offer courses in environmental engineering.

ENGINEERING

RACE ENGINEER

AN ENGINEERING QUALIFICATION CAN TAKE YOU INTO THE SUPER-FAST WORLD OF MOTOR RACING.

For any fans of car racing there is nothing as exciting as a Formula One race. The drivers competing against each other in Grand Prix races are in cars that often reach speeds of more than 350 km/h. One of the most important members of every race team is the race engineer. As a race engineer, your main job will be to make sure that the car is set up to suit conditions and tactics, and that it performs at its best during the race.

▲ The data you collect and study from the on-board computers will tell the team of mechanics how to set up different parts of the car, including the aerodynamic wings.

WHAT YOU DO

Outside of the race season, you will be involved in developing and testing the car for the next season. When the races begin, your job will involve setting the car up for practice and qualification, checking data from on-board computers to see how it performs and then deciding with the team how to get the most out of the car.

▶ Throughout the race, race engineers listen to the driver to find out how the car is handling.

WHERE YOU WORK

The companies that build Formula One cars are called 'constructors' and many of the best race engineers work for one of them. However, you could choose to work for a company that provides engines or other parts for the constructors.

SCHOOL: Maths, science and computing

THE ROUTE TO

SENIOR SCHOOL: Maths, science (especially physics), computing and engineering

RACE ENGINEERING

UNIVERSITY: Mechanical engineering, automotive engineering or electrical engineering

▲ Talking to the driver before and after the race and between practice sessions could help you extract more performance from the car.

MAKING BODY PARTS

BUILDING AND ENGINEERING NEW AND REPLACEMENT BODY PARTS CAN HELP PEOPLE REBUILD THEIR LIVES.

Bioengineers help to design and build artificial replacements for body parts that are either missing or not functioning properly. One of the main areas that bioengineers work in is the development of artificial limbs. These are called prosthetics. Some prosthetics even have electronics in them that can react to instructions given to them by the wearer. Engineers are also trying to develop artificial limbs that can respond to the wearer's thoughts.

◄ An engineer adjusts the settings on a prosthetic leg in the laboratory before it is sent to the person who will wear it.

SOME PEOPLE WITH DISABILITIES ARE STILL KEEN TO CARRY ON TAKING PART IN SPORTS. IF YOU WANT TO WORK IN SPORTS AND BIOENGINEERING THEN YOU CAN BE INVOLVED IN THE DEVELOPMENT OF THE SPECIALIST ARTIFICIAL LIMBS USED BY ATHLETES.

IT IS NOW POSSIBLE TO REPLACE OTHER PARTS OF THE BODY, INCLUDING INTERNAL ORGANS SUCH AS THE HEART, LIVER AND KIDNEYS. BIOENGINEERS ARE ALSO WORKING ON REPLACEMENTS FOR SKIN, INTESTINES AND BONES.

WHAT YOU DO

Much of your working day will be spent in the laboratory working as part of a team researching and developing artificial body parts. Some of your day will be away from the laboratory, as you will probably have to meet both the patient and the medical team who are working with them.

WHERE YOU WORK

There are healthcare companies that create artificial body parts and it is likely that you will be working for one of these companies. You could also be working for hospitals or for medical schools that specialise in bioengineering.

◄ A sprinter with a specially designed prosthetic running leg powers away at the start of a race.

THE ROUTE
TO BIOENGINEERING

SCHOOL: Maths, science and computing

SENIOR SCHOOL: Maths, science (especially biology), computing and engineering

UNIVERSITY: Biomedical engineering or mechanical engineering

DRILLING ENGINEER

FIND OUT WHAT IT TAKES TO DRILL DEEP INTO THE EARTH'S INTERIOR.

The world needs energy and, at the moment, over half of all our energy comes from oil and gas. Both are buried in large underground fields and have to be extracted by drilling. As a drilling engineer, you will help to discover these new fields around the world. This means that you will have to have some knowledge of geology. You will then need to organise test drillings and, if these are successful, you will be involved in building the wells needed to bring the oil and gas to the surface.

THE DEEPEST FLOATING OIL PLATFORM IS THE *PERDIDO* WHICH SITS IN 2,450 METRES OF WATER IN THE GULF OF MEXICO.

▲ A drilling engineer analyses the earth and rock brought up by drilling and keeps a record in a 'mud log'.

WHAT YOU DO

The working day of a drilling engineer may take you to many different parts of the world as you will be responsible for the building of wells. Oil and gas fields are being found in some of the most challenging environments in the world. Many of the new fields are being found out at sea, so you will probably spend some of your time on an oil or gas platform far from land.

DRILLING ENGINEERS ARE ALSO INVOLVED IN TRYING TO MEET THE WORLD'S INCREASING DEMAND FOR WATER. THIS WATER IS OFTEN FOUND BY DRILLING INTO UNDERGROUND SOURCES OF WATER CALLED AQUIFERS.

▼ Drilling platforms can be found far out to sea, boring through the ocean floor to reach the oil and gas.

WHERE YOU WORK

The exploration of new oil and gas fields is mostly in the hands of big energy companies. They are continually searching for new fields around the world and most drilling engineers work for one of these big companies. There are also some smaller companies who specialise in the design and building of oil and gas wells.

THE ROUTE

SCHOOL: Maths, science and computing

SENIOR SCHOOL: Maths, science (especially biology), geography and engineering

TO DRILLING ENGINEER

UNIVERSITY: Petroleum engineering, mechanical engineering or civil engineering

SPORTS SHOE ENGINEER

CAN YOU ENGINEER THE NEXT BIG THING IN SPORTS EQUIPMENT?

If you want to be a top-class athlete then you'll need to be fit and healthy and ready to put in the practice. However, lots of athletes are also turning to technology to help improve their performance and engineers can help, especially when it comes to what they wear on their feet. As a sports shoe engineer, you'll be involved in creating general purpose shoes for the everyday runner, as well as specialist footwear for elite athletes in different sports.

▲ A good general running shoe should support the athlete's foot and provide cushioning to absorb impact.

◄ Studying how a person runs is called gait analysis and it well help you to create shoes that could improve their performance.

WHAT YOU DO

As a sports shoe engineer you will be dividing your time between researching and experimenting on your shoes. To help you with this you will study how athletes run and then use Computer-Aided Design (CAD) to create a digital model. Once a shoe has been created, you will also see how athletes use it and get their feedback on how well the shoe performs.

WHERE YOU WORK

Most sports shoe engineers work for one of the large companies that design and manufacture all sorts of sports clothes and equipment. Many of these companies have offices across the globe, so you may find yourself working in different countries.

THE ROUTE TO

SCHOOL: Maths, science and computing

SENIOR SCHOOL: Maths, science (especially biology and physics), engineering and design

SPORTS SHOE ENGINEERING

UNIVERSITY: Sports engineering or mechanical engineering

A CAREER IN SPORTS ENGINEERING COULD LEAD TO A JOB WORKING WITH ALL SORTS OF SPORTS EQUIPMENT, INCLUDING IMPROVING TENNIS RACKETS OR MAKING SWIMSUITS THAT REDUCE FRICTION.

MAKING TOYS

IF YOU BELIEVED PLAYTIME STOPPED WHEN YOU GREW UP, THEN THIS JOB WILL MAKE YOU THINK AGAIN!

When a toy is designed and built, somebody with engineering skills will be part of the team. As a toy engineer, you will be involved in making sure that all parts of the toy work efficiently and that the toy itself is fun to use. One of your most important jobs will be to use your engineering skills to make sure that any new toys are safe. It will be up to you to engineer the toy so that no small parts can be taken off and swallowed.

◄ Many modern toys use computer chips that allow them to interact with their owners.

◄ The Rubik's Cube was created by architecture professor Ernö Rubik to help his students understand 3-D objects.

AS A TOY ENGINEER, YOU MAY BE ABLE TO SPECIALISE IN THE KIND OF TOYS BEING CREATED. YOU MIGHT WANT TO JUST CONCENTRATE ON ACTION TOYS OR TOYS FOR BABIES.

THE ROUTE TO TOY ENGINEERING

SCHOOL: Maths, science, computing and art

SENIOR SCHOOL: Maths, science (especially physics), engineering and design

UNIVERSITY: Electrical engineering or mechanical engineering

19

WHERE YOU WORK

If you want to work in toy engineering then you will probably work for a toy manufacturer. Many of these are creating toys that can be sold all over the world so you will have the chance to work in several different countries. There are also some companies that design toys but do not make them. If you work for one of these companies then you will be part of a team that will try to sell the designs to a toy manufacturer.

▼ A toy fair is a good place to see the other toys appearing on the market.

WHAT YOU DO

If you are developing a new toy then you will be part of a team and you will have to work closely with them through every stage in the creation of a new toy. When you are working on the design of the toy, you will be using a computer a lot to help you with your work. Once you are testing the toy then you'll spend much more time in a laboratory or in toy shops watching how children use your creations.

BUILDING SHIPS

▼ As well as building new ships, your role may involve repairing or refitting existing ships to bring them up-to-date.

POWERING THE SHIPS THAT SAIL AROUND THE GLOBE TAKES SOME SUPER-ADVANCED ENGINEERING.

There are lots of types of ship out at sea right now. These include bulk carriers, cargo and container ships, tankers carrying oil and gas, and enormous cruise ships. All of these ships need the skills of an engineer to keep them running efficiently and safely. As a ship engineer you will be involved in designing and building new ships, ensuring that they can perform safely and efficiently.

◄ Many ships are built in sections that are then joined together at the shipyard.

WHAT YOU DO

When you are at the initial design stage of engineering a ship then you will be based in an office using CAD software. However, you will also have to spend a lot of time away from your desk supervising the building, maintenance or repair of ships at the shipyard.

IF YOU WANT TO BE RESPONSIBLE FOR THE DESIGN OF THE WHOLE SHIP, THEN YOU WILL HAVE TO RETURN TO UNIVERSITY TO CARRY ON STUDYING MARINE ENGINEERING AT A HIGHER LEVEL.

WHERE YOU WORK

Most ship engineers work for ship building companies that are based at shipyards. You could also work for companies that specialise in the repair and maintenance of ships. Countries with large navies, such as the Royal Navy in the UK or the United States Navy, employ engineers to work on their ships.

SCHOOL: Maths, science and computing

THE ROUTE TO

SENIOR SCHOOL: Maths, science (especially physics), engineering and design

BUILDING SHIPS

UNIVERSITY: Marine engineering, electrical engineering or mechanical engineering

SKYSCRAPER ENGINEERING

THIS JOB WILL LET YOU REACH FOR THE SKY AS YOU CREATE SOME OF THE WORLD'S TALLEST BUILDINGS.

Major cities around the world build towering skyscrapers to create more living and working space. These huge buildings provide massive engineering challenges. As a skyscraper engineer, your most important task is to make sure that the skyscraper stays standing up after it's built. You will have to understand how the building's materials will cope with the stresses and strains of life high above the city streets.

THE SHARD IN LONDON IS 309.6 METRES TALL AND HAS ENOUGH GLASS TO COVER EIGHT FOOTBALL PITCHES.

WHAT YOU DO

At the start of a project you will be spending your time in your office using a computer to work on the design of every part of the skyscraper. You will also set up computer models to test the parts of the skyscraper you are responsible for. Some testing will also have to be done in a laboratory. When the skyscraper is being built, you will have to be on site to help supervise the engineering work needed.

▲ You will work closely with the architect to make sure the building fulfils their vision and is safe to use.

THERE ARE MANY SPECIALIST ROLES INVOLVED IN BUILDING A SKYSCRAPER. THESE INCLUDE DESIGNING THE ELEVATORS, AIR-CONDITIONING, LIGHTING AND THE SUPPLY OF WATER TO ALL FLOORS.

SCHOOL: Maths, science and computing

THE ROUTE TO

SENIOR SCHOOL: Maths, science (especially physics), engineering and design

SKYSCRAPER

UNIVERSITY: Civil engineering or mechanical engineering

ENGINEERING

WHERE YOU WORK

If you decide to work on the engineering of skyscrapers then you will have a choice about the kind of business that you work for. You may work for a large architectural company that is responsible for all parts of the building of the skyscraper. You could also work for an engineering company that specialises in providing engineering expertise to building projects.

◀ The Burj Khalifa in Dubai, UAE, is currently the world's tallest building and stands 828 metres high.

THRILLS AND SPILLS

IF ROLLER COASTER THRILLS ARE YOUR THING, THEN THIS IS THE JOB FOR YOU!

As a roller coaster engineer, you will have to decide on what the roller coaster will look like. That means making decisions about the height of any drops, whether there will be any water or tunnels and if there are going to be any vertical loops. You will have to use your engineering skills to decide on the upper speed limit of the cars on the roller coaster. You'll need an understanding of how the materials used on the roller coaster work and you will also need a good knowledge of physics and even know something about the human body.

◄ Some modern roller coasters are built using traditional materials, such as wood.

WHAT YOU DO

Although you will spend some time in the office working on the design of the roller coaster, you will also be at the amusement park itself to make sure that the engineering work is done properly. You will have the chance to do a test ride of the roller coaster yourself. However, this is usually done when the amusement park is closed, so you may find yourself taking a ride at night.

THE ROUTE TO

SCHOOL: Maths, science and computing

SENIOR SCHOOL: Maths, science (especially physics), engineering and design

ROLLER COASTER ENGINEERING

UNIVERSITY: Electrical engineering civil engineering or mechanical engineering

WHERE YOU WORK

Some of the bigger amusement parks employ their own roller coaster engineers. They mostly work on the maintenance of the rides that are already there. There are also engineering companies that specialise in designing and building new roller coasters.

▼ Modern roller coaster designs put riders through extreme moves, including loops and corkscrews.

THE FASTEST ROLLER COASTER IS FORMULA ROSSA AT FERRARI WORLD IN THE UAE, WHICH ZOOMS ALONG AT 240 KM/H.

ENGINEERING AIRCRAFT

FIND OUT WHAT IT TAKES TO GET THE WIND BENEATH YOUR WINGS.

▼ The Boeing 787 Dreamliner is built from composite materials, making it lighter and more fuel efficient than other airliners.

Aircraft, or aeronautical, engineers work on the design, building and maintenance of all sorts of aircraft. They design the shape of an aircraft so that it will take off, fly through the air and land. They also make sure that the aircraft is fitted with the right engines, and other systems, such as navigation and communication. Above all, they need to make sure that the aircraft is safe and complies with many international regulations.

◄ Some aeronautical engineers are involved in the creation of experimental aircraft, such as this X-43 scramjet tested by NASA.

WHAT YOU DO

As an aeronautical engineer, you will spend some time in your office, but there are plenty of times when you will be working elsewhere. You will be in the workshops where the parts of the aircraft are being made or in the hangers where all of the parts are put together. You will also be in the laboratory testing aircraft parts.

AERONAUTICAL ENGINEERS ARE AN IMPORTANT PART OF A CRASH INVESTIGATION TEAM. THEY HELP TO WORK OUT HOW THE CRASH HAPPENED, SO THAT SIMILAR ACCIDENTS CAN BE AVOIDED.

WHERE YOU WORK

Most aeronautical engineers work for companies that design and build aircraft. Airline operators also employ their own aeronautical engineers. If you work for an airline operator, then much of your working day will be on the maintenance of the aircraft the operator owns.

◀ Using the latest design technology and materials, future airliners may look very different from those used today.

THE ROUTE TO
AERONAUTICAL ENGINEERING

SCHOOL: Maths, science and computing

SENIOR SCHOOL: Maths, science and engineering

UNIVERSITY: Aeronautical or aerospace engineering, electrical engineering or mechanical engineering

BUILDING BRIDGES

CUTTING-EDGE ENGINEERING TECHNOLOGY IS USED TO CROSS RIVERS, VALLEYS AND GORGES.

Your work as a bridge engineer will start well before the design and engineering begins, selecting the correct location, taking into account many variables such as the local geology and weather conditions. You will also have to work with models, usually computer-generated, before the real thing is actually built. As a bridge engineer you will also have to make sure that your bridges can survive not only the daily use of pedestrians, car or trains but also extreme weather conditions such as hurricanes or tornadoes.

THE DANYANG-KUNSHAN GRAND BRIDGE IS THE LONGEST IN THE WORLD, STRETCHING FOR NEARLY 165 KM.

THE ROUTE TO BRIDGE ENGINEERING

SCHOOL: Maths, science and computing

SENIOR SCHOOL: Maths, science, computing and engineering

UNIVERSITY: Structural or civil engineering

A BRIDGE IN CHINA IS KNOWN LOCALLY AS 'BRAVE MAN'S BRIDGE' BECAUSE THE WALKWAY IS MADE OF GLASS, GIVING USERS A SCARY VIEW OF THE VALLEY FLOOR SOME 180 METRES BELOW.

▶ A CAD model of a bridge allows engineers to test designs and materials before anything has been built.

WHERE YOU WORK

If you want to work in bridge engineering then you will probably work for a company that specialises in civil engineering projects. Some engineers also work for rail companies or for national organisations that maintain roads. Whoever you work for you will be working with other engineers and with non–engineers, such as designers and architects.

▼ The Milau Viaduct in France is the tallest bridge in the world, with towers reaching 343 metres high.

WHAT YOU DO

Bridge engineers divide their time between their office, the laboratory and being at the site where the bridge is located. In the office you will spend your time working on the engineering needed for a new bridge. This will include creating computer models to test how the bridge will work. In the laboratory, you will help in the construction of models to carry on with testing. You will supervise the building of the bridge and may also be involved in checking the bridge at regular intervals after its opening.

GLOSSARY

ADDITIVE MANUFACTURING
Another term for 3-D printing, it refers to how objects are made by adding material, such as plastic and metal, rather than by starting with a large block of material and cutting pieces away to make the object.

AERODYNAMICS
The study of how air moves around solid objects.

AERONAUTICAL
Related to the design and study of machines that can fly.

AMUSEMENT PARK
A large park that contains rides, such as roller coasters, and stalls to entertain people.

AQUIFER
An underground layer of rock that contains a store of water and can be used to supply wells.

ARCHITECT
A person who designs buildings.

BIOENGINEER
A person who designs replacement body parts, such as artificial limbs.

CIVIL ENGINEERING
The design and building of large engineering projects, such as harbours, roads, bridges and public buildings.

CLIMATE CHANGE
The change in Earth's overall climate which many scientists believe is being caused by human activities.

COMPUTER-AIDED DESIGN
Using computer software and graphics to design objects, such as cars, aircraft and buildings.

DOCTORATE
One of the highest qualifications you can receive.

FORMULA ONE
The highest class of motor racing for professional drivers.

FRICTION
A force produced when one substance rubs against another.

GAIT ANALYSIS
The study of how a person walks or runs, it is used to see how an athlete can improve their performance.

GEOLOGY
The study of the history and structure of Earth, in particular its rocks.

GORGES
A very steep-sided valley that's usually formed by the eroding actions of a river.

GRAND PRIX
The races that make up a season in Formula One motor racing.

GREENHOUSE GASES
The gases that add to the greenhouse effect and may cause climate change.

HYDROELECTRIC POWER
Electricity that's generated by the movement of water.

MASTER'S DEGREE
A university degree that is a higher level than a first, or bachelor's, degree.

MUD LOG
A record of the earth and rock brought to the surface by drilling.

NAVIGATION
The ability to find your location and plot a route to another location.

PROSTHETIC
Artificial body parts that are used to replace natural ones that are damaged or have been lost.

REGULATIONS
Rules and principles that govern how something should behave.

RENEWABLE ENERGY
Electricity that is produced from sources that won't run out, such the wind, waves and sunlight.

ROLLER COASTER
Open cars that run on rails and go through a series of moves intended to thrill or scare the riders, such as steep drops, loops and corkscrews.

SCRAMJET
A type of jet engine that is designed to cope with very fast speeds.

SHIPYARD
A place where ships are built, maintained or repaired.

SOLAR FARM
Also known as a photovoltaic power station, this is an area of land that is covered with solar cells which generate electricity from sunlight.

TURBINE
A large wheel that is made up of a series of blades.

VIADUCT
A bridge that carries a road or railway across a valley.

WIND TURBINE
A generator that produces electricity when the wind turns its bladed wheel.

INDEX